**ANCHOR BOOKS**

MEMORIES FROM WITHIN

Edited by

Simon Harwin

First published in Great Britain in 2003 by
ANCHOR BOOKS
Remus House,
Coltsfoot Drive,
Peterborough, PE2 9JX
Telephone (01733) 898102

All Rights Reserved

Copyright Contributors 2003

SB ISBN 1 84418 252 5

FOREWORD

Anchor Books is a small press, established in 1992, with the aim of promoting readable poetry to as wide an audience as possible.

We hope to establish an outlet for writers of poetry who may have struggled to see their work in print.

The poems presented here have been selected from many entries, and as always editing proved to be a difficult task.

I trust this selection will delight and please the authors and all those who enjoy reading poetry.

Simon Harwin
Editor

CONTENTS

Change For A Shilling	Elaine Beresford	1
When I Was Young	M Wills	2
Tears Of A Clown	Rachel Mary Mills	3
Lavender Hills	Andrew James	4
Mortality	Carol Pearce	5
The Classroom	Floyd Coggins	6
For My Daughter	M Sanderson	7
Words Shot Me Instead	Graham Hare	8
Blackberrying	Mollie D Earl	9
Mother's Day	Sophie Jordanov	10
J Lo Limerick	A Sackey	11
My Favourite Isle	Lachlan Taylor	12
The Good Old Days	Rosemary Davies	13
The Old Forge	John Mitchell	14
The Mists Of Time	Joan Magennis	15
Down Memory Lane	Geoffrey S S Wilyman	16
Remembering Friends	Alan Millard	17
Why?	R D Hiscoke	18
Hearing Them Talk About The Forties	Kathleen Mary Scatchard	19
For Norma	Beryl Moorehead	20
Supermarkets	Mary Tickle	21
Childhood Memories Of Winter	Albert E Bird	22
Behold That Distant Star	I T Hoggan	24
Look Back In Time	Jeanette Gaffney	25
My Childhood Pet	J F Grainger	26
Washing Day	Jack Bowden	27
Memories Of Childhood Summers	Margaret M Donnelly	28
My Kite	Diane Bowen	30
London (Home)	Dan Del'ouest	31
A Walk Back - 50 Years	Janet Cavill	32
A True Heart	Malcolm Peter Mansfield	33
The Memory Box	Irene Siviour	34
Jukebox Lament	Paul Kelly	36
Johanna	Rona Laycock	37

A Backward Glance	Gladys C'Ailceta	38
Memories	Joan Cashford	39
Remembering	Violet Willis	40
How I Miss You, Mother Of Mine	Nicky Young	42
A Trip To Memory Lane	Jean P McGovern	44
A Dream	D Gilson	45
Through The Eyes Of A Child	Linda Constantatos	46
Skegness	Megan Ward	47
I Remember	Joan Prentice	48
The Old Iford Bridge	Sammy Michael Davis	49
Country Schoolboy	Terry O'Reilly	50
Haymaking	Bernadette McQuaid-Murphy	51
Fantasies Don't Breed Memories	Darren Hobson	52
Friends Departed	Dorothy Mary Allchin	53
Geraldine's Memories	Geraldine McMullan Doherty	54
The Ballad Of Walham Green	Jo Brookes	56
Memories	E D Bowen	57
Margate - 1946	Marian F Delfgou	58
At Play In Yesterday	I R Finch	59
Childhood Memories	Alison Czajkowski	60
Coco School	Muriel Mackay	61
Memories Past And Present	Leslie Trotter	62
Childhood	Ellen Thompson	63
My Brother Tom	Harry Skinn	64
Sisters	Valerie Walton	65
Childhood Summers	Jane Otieno	66
Childhood Holidays	Colin Jones	68
Town Hall Park	P S D MacArthur	70
Better Than	Lynn Mottram	71
Childhood Memories	Audrey Davies	72
The Saturday Penny	Margaret B Baguley	73
The Arches	B Page	74
Where Have All The Days Gone?	Kerri Morehu-Baker	75
Sausages	Jax Burgess	76
The Street Where I Was Born	A F Mace	77
Thoughts From Childhood	John Paulley	78
The Good Old Bad Days	B Cotterill	79

Title	Author	Page
Seems Like Yesterday . . .	Jo-Ann Waldron-Hall	80
Christmas Eve	Gaye Gatehouse	82
Big Head	Esmond Hannon	83
This Game	Rebecca Johnson	84
Nightmares Of Childhood	David Bridgewater	85
Sweet Shop Down The Lane	Louise Mawbey	86
Covert Boyhood	Patrick Brady	87
Tins, Tambourines And A Big Bass Drum	David Muncaster	88
A Child's Wonderland	Patricia Carter	89
Childhood Memories	Kathleen Holmes	90
The Stream	Mike Curtis	91
70s Remembered	Martin Kerr	92
Childhood Memories	Maureen Anderson	93
School Blues	John Black	94
For My Nanny	J Gatenby	95
Those Happy Days	Leslie Frank Checkley	96
Those Bygone Days	Tess Walton	98
Hunstanton	Joyce M Jones	100
The Road	Kinsman Clive	101
Lost Childhood	Diana Richardson	102
Unborn	Sharon Simpson	103
The Bluebell Woods - May 1948	Frances Marie Cecelia Harvey	104
Remembrance Of Childhood	Harry Crompton-Fils	106
An Insignificance Of Being	Anthony Ross-Fallon	107
Childhood Holidays	Pat Rogers	108
The Secret	Valerie Catterall	109
I Don't Understand Why	Sue Elle	110

CHANGE FOR A SHILLING

Singing, she skipped along the pier,
Clutching the silver shilling in her hand,
As she headed for the brightly lit arcade,
Her summer shoes full of drying sand.

Ernie, well-loved by all the children,
Retired from a sailor's life at sea,
Gave change for the penny slot machines,
Enjoying the youthful company.

Bright-eyed, she asked him for twelve coppers,
Handing him her shilling with a smile,
They chatted as he dipped into his leather bag,
And felt a kind of sadness for a while.

She pulled the enormous metal handle,
Oranges and lemons began to spin,
She scooped the clattering pennies as they fell,
But in the end, machines would always win.

All week she came with her new shillings
Changed by Ernie, her good friend,
With tearful goodbye on the Saturday,
When her holiday came to an end.

Her mother gently broke the news,
That Ernie had been ill and passed away,
Sweet memories of change for a shilling,
As part of her childhood died that day.

Elaine Beresford

WHEN I WAS YOUNG

Oh how I miss when I was young,
No stress and problem free,
To wander anywhere,
Come and go as I pleased.

Parties, dances, records too,
Making friends with someone new,
Chewing gum and motorbikes,
Discos with flashing lights.

Denim jeans, Top of the Pops,
Dancing the whole night through,
Mini skirts and back-combed hair,
Nylons and pointed shoes.

Such happy days,
Way back then,
Life was full of fun,
Oh how I miss when I was young.

M Wills

TEARS OF A CLOWN

Do you have toys you girls and boys?
If you're young or getting old,
Do you treasure that lovely teddy?
Well I've a poem to be told.

I have a teddy called 'Sunny',
He was bought on a sunny day,
I got him in Barnardo's shop,
And he's here with me to stay.

And I've also a clown, he has pink hair,
And he's dressed in white, pinks and green!
I called him Marco, he sleeps all day,
Was this to be foreseen?

He came from the same shop as Sunny,
Date 11.9.01. I'll never forget that awful day,
When that evil thing was done.

And my memories will stay forever,
Although I knew no one there,
Marco sleeps the day away,
Beside Sunny in the chair.

And at night I let them hold hands you see,
And I whisper a little prayer,
God bless you all from Twin Towers,
You are all in God's loving care.

Rachel Mary Mills

LAVENDER HILLS

If I could paint a memory,
A sound enticed by sight of
Wet roses and dew-dropped lilies,
It would be of painted memories of you.
If we were together underneath the orange clouds
Would you sing me a song that shows how you see?
Too deep with aroma, the garden where we sit.
Time stops the water flowing down the stream.
Too many sparks cloud my dreams,
I stir heat into my pillows as lavender-painted hands cover my eyes.
Give me your hands and paint your face
Where you stand in lavenders, hazed by plum
Then let the fires blaze and take me away.

I often tread those thoughts of time that stops the poppies growing.
Shadows move my feet,
Whilst the crying I tear makes no change.
My hair is cut and thrown in a bin,
All I ask is for your hands but strapped to a bed,
The sunset dawns the end of the day.
Where is your nearness when I need conversations?
Dappled lights refract on my face.
Walk away as usual,
The light you see is cinders of lavender
Purple skies made illumina burn coldly,
Deceitful you are, pushing me in your burning arson of lavender
Try harder to visualise that they took me away.
However,
Your hands are my eyes lost in a lavender hill painting.

Andrew James (15)

MORTALITY

Even after all this time there's a void that's buried deep
Memories that flood my mind which make me want to weep.
Such sadness washes over me with a pain that's hard to bear
When I think of all the years gone by when you've not been there.
You went to sleep too soon for me; we didn't say goodbye
And countless times I look above and ask the question, 'Why?'
I ached for you to guide me in my first years as a wife
And part of me died with you when you let go of life.
I needed you to let me know if I was doing right or wrong
And missed you more than ever when my children came along.
You would have revelled in their childhood;
A bonding would have grown
But it was not to be that way - and I wish that I had known . . .
If only we could see the future; what adjustments we would make
Absorbing every moment along the paths we take.

Carol Pearce

My mum and dad Brighton 1950

The Classroom

As I look around me, my heart is filled with envy
Happy faces waiting patiently to embark on life's great journey
That sense of evolving aspirations and untapped ambition
That represents all that I once said and all that I once did.
But oh what treasures I would trade, if just one more, I could be a kid.

Floyd Coggins

FOR MY DAUGHTER

Twenty-five short years ago
A baby shared our life
And now before our very eyes
She's turned into a wife.

I hope that through these years she's learned
Honour, trust and truth
To temper, with new-found wisdom
The impulsiveness of youth.

The hardest job's to stand aside
And learn to let you go
But if you think I made mistakes
It's because I loved you so.

So be happy darling daughter
In the life that's yours to lead
My love is yours forever
Whatever you may need.

M Sanderson

WORDS SHOT ME INSTEAD
(Dedicated to Faye)

I'll never forget those final
parting words you spoke

if only it had been a joke

your hate and pain still remains
so you inflicted yours into my brain

I know we'll never be the same

but who is to blame
still your old flame?

For a love that burned so bright
you so suddenly snuffed out our light

spoken with such violent intent
showing no mercy or even regret

in just one moment our love was spent

as if you'd shot me in the head
while we were both still in our bed.

Graham Hare

BLACKBERRYING

In August hols or coming days
Of a misty September morn
Down the blackberry lanes would we all go
Not far from where we were born.

We'd work along the bramble hedge
To select the ripest and the best
We ate as many as we could
The birds could have the rest!

We tried to reach the highest fruits
We tried and tried in vain
Always the best ones out of reach
Down the blackberry lane.

We'd fill our baskets full of fruit
The black and juicy ones
Altho' a few of half ripe reds
Could be found amongst the tons.

We'd scratch our hands and tear our clothes
But oh we had some fun
It was a special kind of joy
When all is said and done.

We'd take the baskets home to Mum
With blackberries brimming o'er
And Mum would make us jam and pies
Mixed with apples from the store.

Just doing things that children do
To while away the day
When holidays were long and sweet
And we had time to play.

Mollie D Earl

MOTHER'S DAY
*(For my mother, Katrina, with love and hugs,
from Sophie, Dan, Erik, Jack and Ebo!)*

Mothers, you'll find, grow like leaves on trees,
But that's where the simile ends.
Who else do you know who will bend like a reed,
When you ask her a favour again?
She'll type up your letters and look round the shops
For something you've asked her to find.
Even your friends, who like you a lot,
Would not be so repeatedly kind!
She doesn't expect very much in return,
Which can be problematic when
You realise you're starting to take her for granted
And being too selfish again.
But luckily for all those children like me,
There comes once a year such a date;
Called Mothering Sunday, when we all show our mummies
That they're one in a million and great!

Sophie Jordanov

J LO LIMERICK

There's a popular singer called J Lo
Who delightfully sways to and fro
It's not only her voice
That makes many rejoice
It's her bottom that often steals the show.

A Sackey

My Favourite Isle

Of all the isles off Scotland's shore
    the one I love the best
Is Skye which I think is wonderful
    and way above the rest

I've spent many a holiday here
    and enjoyed some happy hours
I have never ever been let down
    even with days of rainy showers

The community are all friendly
    and let you know the beauty spots
With lovely coves and sandy bays
    you make sure they're not forgot

Then you have the castle of McLeod
    Dunvegan is its name
Here visitors get a conducted tour
    to see things of historic fame

Flora McDonald fled to the isle of Skye
    along with the young Pretender
To escape the troops of Cumberland
    who was the Protestant King's defender

Lachlan Taylor

THE GOOD OLD DAYS

When I was young and small,
I thought everyone seemed tall.
There was always time to kick a ball,
And no one locked their doors at all.

In those days the neighbours all got on,
We would get together for a sing-along.
Children were taught right from wrong,
And discipline was extremely strong.

We enjoyed the simple pleasures in life,
A day out at the seaside with the wife.
We lived in a world without much strife,
Muggings and murder weren't so rife.

Jobs were plentiful way back then,
Heads of households were always men.
We grew vegetables in the garden,
And had new laid eggs from our hen.

I was always awake with the lark,
And went to bed when it was dark.
I liked working as an office clerk,
And I enjoyed strolling in the park.

We had perfect summer weather,
Families used to eat together.
Our shoes were made of leather,
I really was as light as a feather!

Oh yes, I remember those days well,
Such wonderful stories I could tell!

Rosemary Davies

THE OLD FORGE

The old thatched smithy livened the tranquil street,
With ringing anvil, calling the hostlers to meet.
The bearded blacksmith in his leather apron torn,
Mastered his craft with a keen eye and brawn.

Dry sticks kindled the forge till drawing,
Great bellows fanned the coals till roaring.
Anvil sings 'neath hammer blows not missing,
On white-hot metal with sparks all hissing.

Tireless he pumped to keep the fire bright,
Heating shapeless irons for the hammer's strike.
Gnarled hands hold the iron on the anvil's shoulder,
Under a frenzy of blows and sparks that smoulder.

His skills ranged from shoeing a horse's hoof,
To making wrought iron gates for gents aloof.
Straightening plough beams, and axles true,
Repairing implements and tools to look like new.

As the heat and smoke cleared at the end of the day,
He'd enjoy his ale brought from across the way.
Over the years his skills were no longer required,
Machines in factories made all that was desired.

Long gone now, the smithy and his smoking beard,
All his tools and anvil have long been cleared.
The old forge now has carpets, curtains and trimming,
Hark, sometimes you can hear a ghostly anvil ringing!

John Mitchell

THE MISTS OF TIME

I watch the days of long ago
In the flickering firelight's glow
Where memories that are golden-lined
Burn ever brightly on my mind
Shadows dance upon the wall
The sparks crack a familiar sounding call

It's Mammy calling me by name
Her sweet voice is just the same
With the flames I see her face colliding
I feel she's there, my thoughts guiding
The fire burns brightly, we embrace
We meet in flames, face to face

We laugh and smile, for we're together
We walk in flames in sunny weather
The daydream fades, in the embers there
I shake myself in the fireside chair
Forever captured in the words of rhyme
Are memories lost in the mists of time

Joan Magennis

Down Memory Lane

Oh how we lived in days gone by
No radios, TV, work hours to fly
Until half-day, the village dance
Polished shoes, band, perchance

No squealing voices or microphone
Well-trained voice, never a moan
Neatly dressed, girls all in dresses
Never allowed, sex, one confesses

Hair-dos on males always cut short
Grey flannel shirts, jackets for sport
Girls, long dresses, petticoats galore
Sequinned beauties to adore

We danced and sang to Saturday night
All such harmony, seldom a fight
Singing, dancing, eight 'til eleven
In those days, life, dancing heaven!

In luck, a kiss to say goodnight
Fox trots, waltzes, changed partners tight!
Valetas, trumpets, steps so light,
Speedily passed dance band night!

Geoffrey S S Wilyman

REMEMBERING FRIENDS

I thought you'd always be there,
Sometimes like a headache,
Sometimes like a comfortable chair,
But always there to make
Things happen, break the day,
Share a cup of tea
And while away
The hour from two till three
With little more
Than talk of things we'd talked about
Before
And would again, no doubt,
At times, we had our funny ways,
Said things that, later, we'd regret,
And even wished on off-days
That we'd never met,
And yet, you always came,
Each day at two,
And always the same
Old you
And me?
I thought you'd always be there,
That I'd never see,
As now, only your empty chair.

Alan Millard

Why?

Tears have stained my pillow as they, for you, are shed
Leaving so suddenly, as the doctor pronounced you dead
You were not ill, how could this be? A picture of good health
Struck down without a warning, perhaps this amazed yourself?
You were always such a comfort and those many problems you solved
Your advice and companionship were a treasure to behold
I know our love was sanctified when first you came into my view
We jelled immediately, my darling, as we lived our life so true

You will be missed, my sweetheart, though I still feel you near
Guiding me like you used to, I shall have no fear
Still you will remain with me, it's so comforting to know
But still I shed tears of sorrow, why did you have to go?
Sweet are those wonderful memories, I hold these within my heart
You were my all and from you I could never ever part
You will never be forsaken, but still I ask the question, why
In that state of robust health even an athletic you should up and die?

One day we shall be reunited, oh what happiness there will be
Like a young bride once again in all that finery
You, of course, will be waiting with outstretched arms to enthral
There will be such rejoicing as eternity will conquer all

R D Hiscoke

HEARING THEM TALK ABOUT THE FORTIES

When Snow White inspired those
Castles in the clouds,
Sherbet Dabs,
Rationing, shelters,
Cigarette queues.

Trendy Fantasia,
A sorcerer's apprentice,
Labels were
Not status then, but
Utility.

Mickey Mouse and his friends
Are not age-wearied,
Nor are those
Preserved on film, brave
Images of light.

But now there are new things,
Like the internet,
Pizza Huts,
Pop idols and icons,
Styles in the frame.

Kathleen Mary Scatchard

FOR NORMA

When winter nights enlarge
There is the promise of spring
Tiptoe along the landing
The spiral staircase beckoning

The frozen earth encapsulates
The life beneath the sod
The womb of new beginnings
Preserves the seed of God

Except a grain of wheat doth fall
It abides alone we're told
But if it die the fruit it bears
Will be truly manifold

So it is with our lives
When to return to earth is a must
The spirit of man is best released
When ashes to ashes become
And dust to dust

The spirit is free to soar
Like the eagle on the wing
With strength, freedom of purpose
High above the pine woods
No more the shadow of death
Finished the suffering

Beryl Moorehead

SUPERMARKETS

Going to the supermarkets
What an array
Remembering the days
When we walked a long way
Just to get one item
And maybe queue up
Grateful for a small cut
In this day and age
Speed is of the essence
We have got it nicely made
With a big increase in pay
But some are never happy
They pretend it's all strife
It really is a lot easier
This quick and easy life

Mary Tickle

CHILDHOOD MEMORIES OF WINTER

Give me the winters we had of old,
   When the skies were clear and the nights were cold.
When the stars sparkled bright in the dark night sky,
   And the smoke from the chimney, rose straight up high.

Then in the morning through the frosted panes,
   We looked across the fields and leafless lanes.
With the cold wind from the east, the sun shone all day,
   And there in the shadows, the frost would stay.

Iron-hard was the earth, no ploughs could it break,
   The men with their horses, no work could they make.
The cows in the shippon had to be kept warm,
   With thick straw bedding, they came to no harm.

The water butts froze and icicles were so thick,
   The hens in their pens, no food could they pick.
Our mother would go with some crusts of old bread,
   Crumbled in her hands and so they were fed.

Round the breakfast table we would take our seat,
   With bowls of porridge, with syrup so sweet.
Toast with pork dripping, so thickly spread,
   'You'll come to no harm,' our mother often said.

On our way to the schoolroom, muffled up, we would race,
   With our breath like steam, and a glow on our face.
We'd run into the playground, the slide was still there,
   The faster we could slide, the greater the dare.

Out from the cold and into the classroom so warm,
   The old iron stove that in summer, stood so forlorn,
Was now our centre, we all stood around,
   The register was called and then we all sat down.

The cold would last a fortnight or more,
    The north wind brought snow, it piled up at the door.
And we did those things that we could then only do,
    While brilliant white snow covered the whole country through.

We are older now and those days have gone by,
    The weather has changed and we don't know why.
Sometimes it is too dry or too wet with the rain,
    I wish those winters would come back again.

Albert E Bird

BEHOLD THAT DISTANT STAR

Behold that distant star
That no friendship can mar.
Behold the glorious flowers.
With friends, we wile away the hours.
Behold the radiant moon
And the sandy dune.
Friendship is that rosy wine,
That comes to us from the vine.

I T Hoggan

LOOK BACK IN TIME

When we are older
We look back in time
The days we were young
Seem now so divine
Memories are plentiful
Such wondrous days
Did we do all
Sometimes seen through a haze
Passing on just one or two
Little thoughts
Snippets of knowledge
Not learned from a book
Showing support
When it's needed the most
With love and guidance
Then dreams and new hope
Thinking so differently
From life today
Because all those years
We had memories made
How simply wonderful
All this has been
From young days to old
Where we fulfilled our dreams

Jeanette Gaffney

MY CHILDHOOD PET

When I was young I had this large pet frog
All day he did nothing, he just sat upon a log
His armchair in the pond was a large lily pad
He never seemed very happy, in fact his face was always sad

The colour of my frog was green, he had large staring eyes
For his dinner he had a large helping of flies that passed by
Then one day I found him sitting with another on that lily pad
There are millions of tadpoles swimming, he'd become a dad

The garden pool soon became overcrowded with a lot of baby frogs
They became one big family, they joined their dad sitting on a log
There were so many offspring whose resting place was a lily pad
They had the same expression, they were never happy,
                                        they were always sad

Then a large white bird caught my frog and ate it right away
There was a large choir of frogs croaking thro' the night and day
Soon there be another family of tadpoles who were swimming
                                                    in the pool
Then my friend said making a pet of a frog, I was behaving like a fool

J F Grainger

WASHING DAY

Here in the back lane, in-between yards,
Under this dolly-blue sky, it's washing day.
Mothers punch washing, arms of Popeye,
Soot-covered bricks just crumbling away.

Out of the muck in a crack in the path
Turns a dandelion, stuck, defiant and rare,
Past purple slates, bone chimney pots,
Twists through the clouds to that castle, still there.

Bricks in the yard, deep cobalt and umber,
But not where the sunshine spills from above,
Over black mossy lintels, coal-house and toilet,
Soaks the walls with honey and love.

Milky-blue water flushing in runnels,
Sheets flying and slapping but held by a prop,
Black and tan mongrel flat-out on a proggy-mat,
Cat on the wash-house, hanging, just waiting to drop.

'The bogeyman will get you, he'll eat you all up,'
She warns her little brother, sisterly sweet.
But the bogeyman didn't for he was much too busy
Being bullied by the boys at the bottom of the street.

And now at the top is the rag and bone man,
Smelly horse and balloons, his name on the cart,
Stacked with everything, anything, but nothing at all,
He learned from the clouds his heavenly art.

Jack Bowden

MEMORIES OF CHILDHOOD SUMMERS

In those far-off days of summer
when I was but a child
bringing back those happy memories
safety then, for running wild.

The sun always shone so brightly
or is that in my daydreams?
Sundresses, no socks in sandals,
sunburn, freckles and vanilla ice creams.

An empty glass ginger bottle
filled with water from the tap
rolls wrapped in used waxed bread paper
on our picnic we went with that.

Walking down to the river Avon
we clutched our empty, clean jam jars
hoping to catch some tiny minnows
in those days we had no cars!

My swimsuit wrapped inside a towel
just in case we went for a paddle
we did not have the sunscreen
only calamine lotion in a brown bottle.

My brothers had a branch from a tree
that was to be their fishing rod
a length of string dangling from the end
with this they would catch a cod!

Suffice to say the fish were not biting
so we opened up our lunch
by now, warm water and soggy sandwiches
an easy to please tired bunch

Then while lying on our backs
staring up into the big blue sky
watching the birds high up and soaring
wishing we too could flap our wings and fly.

The girls picking daisies to make a chain
hanging them round their neck and wrist
the boys skimming stones on the water
all this hard work could build of a thirst.

Looking back on those halcyon days of summer
we did not realise we had it made
the most that ever troubled us
was when the sunlight would start to fade!

Margaret M Donnelly

MY KITE

High upon the hilltop,
When the breeze is warm and strong,
I fly my kite with Grandad,
And I hold the string so long.
It's blue and red and box-shaped,
And sweeps up to the sun,
If you've never flown a kite,
You must.
It's awfully jolly fun!

Diane Bowen

LONDON (HOME)

My thoughts of London, are first of home,
Times of fun and friends I'd phone.
We'd make a chain of pretty daisies,
And sit in the sun, just being lazy.
On our rug I'd play with toys,
And some of the local boys.
Around your neck you'd wear the key,
Because you'd come out to play with me.
You came out, we'd go to the market,
And see where the bus would park it.
We would see the parrot shout,
But I was so good, I never got a clout.
I would find it hard to sleep,
But falling from a car seat would help me sleep.
I once had to sleep in my bed, sat up,
And Grandad would bring a hot chocolate cup.
We would buy a cake if we'd brought our money,
I stood on the counter, she didn't find it funny.

Dan Del'ouest

A Walk Back - 50 Years

I took a long walk back in time,
To days so long ago,
I saw the sights that left their name,
For better or for worse.

Men and women older than their years,
Worn down with worry and with work.
Early morning and late night shifts,
Grafted and worked to earn their bread.

Heavy industry brought rewards,
But brought hard work as well,
Few mod cons to light their load,
Holidays not for them.

Yet it was safe to walk the streets,
Children played from dawn till dusk.
Mother chatted at the gate,
To the old man down the street.

Another day, another week,
So much as before,
Just the smell of new baked bread,
To cheer them on their way.

Janet Cavill

A TRUE HEART
(In memory of Olive)

Gone for now -
But your legacy remains.
As evidenced
By the people's lives you did touch
Come together, on this farewell day.
An expression of how loved you were
And are still so . . .
So very, very much.

Even strangers who hardly knew
Could easily sense
Your unconditional care
Free from restriction
And life's enforced chains.

A person of real worth
Right from the start
Right from birth . . .
Such a passion for life
Encompassed by
And contained within
A true heart.

Malcolm Peter Mansfield

THE MEMORY BOX

This time of year I take my time
To reminisce a while
And delve into my memory box
With thoughts of when a child
The air was frosty - bright with stars
At night we would go out
To catch the falling snowflakes
Each one pure and white
We'd make a slide on icy roads
Sing carols of Christmas at doors
A penny often was brought out
And maybe something more
Like home-made toffee - sugar mice
To share between us all.

The gaslight shone on rosy cheeks
As homeward we would go
To stop the cold from taking hold
And sit by the fireside's glow
Into our pockets hands would find
The treasures we all sang for
Then one by one, for you and me
We practised our carols once more.

Tomorrow we go out again
A different street this time
But first to school to make quite sure
The words we sing will rhyme.

As off to bed we go each night
With cocoa drank by candlelight
When Christmas day comes round once more
We find it's gone too soon
So I'll close the lid on my memory box
It's getting far too full
I'll open it up again next year
With treasures still inside
Nostalgic days with beautiful times
What lovely memories then
Let's hope and pray as time goes on
We won't forget the *star of Bethlehem*
So always keep a memory box
It brings such special days
To keep forever in our hearts
That 'time' can never change.

Irene Siviour

JUKEBOX LAMENT

It stands alone in the alcove,
weeping in silence for pity.
Tired, listless, neglected.
Praying for yesterday, hoping
that someone will insert a coin.

It thinks of those days when its
luminous glow and dazzling sheen,
seduced the eager clientele.
When its selection of classics
enticed the wariest of punters.

It smiles fondly, recalling the
money pouring into its slot.
Chuckling wickedly at those gut
busting renditions of 'Hound Dog',
'Lucille' and 'Shakin' All Over'.

A falling coin clinks loudly,
jolting it back to reality.
It grins, waiting patiently,
eager to be pressed into service.
Yet nothing seems to happen.

A fist thumps its glass exterior.
It jumps, shuddering uncontrollably,
grinding slowly into gear.
Lights flickering fitfully,
as it winces from the pain.

The record spins precariously,
groaning in frustration.
A female voice transcends the static.
Connie Francis asks, 'Who's Sorry Now?'
It sighs in resignation.

Paul Kelly

JOHANNA

I remember the day you came to the door
Strange honeyed child with dark brown eyes
I felt pale and awkward in your shadow.
Your confidence came from your seven years
And I was only six.

We played 'pretend' and hopscotch and ball
Your limbs were long and strong.
At night I closed my eyes and dreamt
I was seven and brown and you.
As the years went by I could never catch up
I was always one year behind.

Rona Laycock

A Backward Glance

We relied on home-grown foods when I was young
Apples, pears, blackberries and plums
Potatoes, parsnips, carrots, runner beans
Then of course all the greens.

Chestnuts in the autumn we gathered in
Little food came from a tin
Mushrooms came straight from the fields
Nature willingly giving up her yields.

As for breakfast it was a meal in itself
Eggs, rashers, fried bread, porridge, who cared about health?
Teatime we sat at the table, a typical spread
Jam, cakes, lemon curd and new bread.

At dinner we ate meat with vegetables every day
This was expected, this was the way
Always a pudding, never thought of getting fat
All the exercise did away with that.

Another thing remains in my head
A cup of cocoa and a biscuit before going to bed
Food was our lifeline as it is today
We always said thank you. It's easy to say.

Gladys C'Ailceta

MEMORIES

I miss the paint pots in the shed
The tools in rows on the wall
The smell of creosote
And I miss you most of all

I miss the smell of fresh air on your shirt
The glow on your face after hours of toil
The energy from working on the soil
But I miss you most of all

I miss the enthusiasm of your young face
The challenge you enjoyed and embraced
All systems go, you achieved so much
It's so sad we lost touch
For I miss you so

We are miles apart and old now
I don't know if you are still alive
But I'll always remember you in your shed
Working very hard
And I miss you so.

Joan Cashford

REMEMBERING

Don't ye mind when we were childer runnin' barefoot to the mass,
We hid our sandals in the hedge so that Ma would not get cross.

Don't ye mind we brought the tay down where the men were
                                                                   cuttin' peat,
We took the wee pads through the heather, oh the bliss of dirty feet.

Shure ye mind us playin' marlies with the taws we made of day,
Baked and hardened in the sunshine of a perfect summer day.

You mind the kites we used to make with paper, paste and string,
But mine would always sideways go when we got them on the wing.

In the spring there was the ploughing with the fields all shining white,
For the gulls came in their thousands, it was such a pretty sight.

And of course, ye mind the hayfield when the cocks of hay were made,
With lots of tay and buttermilk an' fresh baked soda bread.

With home-made butter from the churn runnin', meltin'
                                                  round the edge,
An' we sat an' ate jist like a king on the bank beneath the hedge.

Then ye mind we gathered praties in the field behind the spades,
But now it's pratie diggers and such new-fangled aids.

And don't ye mind the harvest an' the cuttin' of the corn,
With spiders' webs dew-spangled on the hedge in early morn.

When we gathered up the sheaves of corn an' stooked them all in rows,
An' Father even showed us how to make our harvest bows.

And then we'd gather blackberries in thon dreadful ten quart cans,
Then tired an' weary, wandered home with purple lips and hands.

And then we'd let the cows out when the milkin' time was done,
Made daisy chains and wore them and troubles we had none.

Oh the memories of our childhood always with us will remain,
Don't you sometimes wish like me that you were just a child again?

Violet Willis

HOW I MISS YOU, MOTHER OF MINE

Oh how I miss you, mother of mine,
you radiated God's light divine.
Through our laughter and our tears,
you loved and guided us through the years.
When we were sick or in pain,
you cared for us till we were well again.
You taught us about sweet Jesus so dear,
for with us He is ever near.
On Mothering Sunday in joyful bliss,
you took our posy with a loving kiss.
If we wandered far or near,
you welcomed us home with a smile and a tear.
If you were ill, to God we did cry,
'Please don't let your angel, our mummy die.'
God delivered you out of your pain,
He'd heard our prayers, you were well again.
Whilst we went through our teenage years,
with love you guided us through joy and tears.
When our marriage vows we did take,
you cried as though your heart would break.
For Mother dear, you loved us so,
it was very hard to see us go.
And when our dearest daddy died,
it broke our hearts to see how you cried.
You missed Daddy so, but we needed you,
God gave you courage and you saw it through.
As the years passed, you became old and frail,
then sadly you began to ail.
We saw your tears now you had to go,
for you knew we would miss you so.
But now you're happy with the one you love,
our saviour, Jesus, in Heaven above.

Oh, how I miss you, sweet mother of mine,
but so joyful are you with the angels divine.
Singing God's praises in Heaven above,
thank you Mother for all of your love.

Nicky Young

A Trip To Memory Lane

As I take you down to memory lane
It will be a pleasure, and never a pain
When the world was young, and at our feet
Thinking of the times so very sweet

My friends would knock for me to play
Especially on a hot summer's day
Playing rounders at the age of eight
Even going to the village fête

Writing numbers, on the pavement floor
Playing hopscotch, competing the highest score
Such fun we knew, of those days of bliss
Running away from boys, who chased us for a kiss

Playing ball against the wall
Taking it in turns when dropping the ball
Three, four, five and six
Juggling the ball, against the bricks

At Christmas time, when the lights were low
Singing carols, on the white virgin snow
Candles were aglow, the Christmas tree alight
As we sang our carols under the pale moonlight

Waking up early on Christmas morn
Celebrating the special day, when Jesus was born
Opening our presents, thankful for what we had
Skipping ropes, puzzle books, board games, gifts from Mum and Dad

Oh what joy it has been for me
Remembering the days, when young and carefree
It's always a pleasure, and never a pain
To take a trip down memory lane

Jean P McGovern

A Dream

Life is like a dream, it does not last
Time to us is only lent
As one gets older, time goes fast
We must make sure every minute is well spent
Just look around at what you own
It may not be much but do not moan
The beauty that God gave us to share
Is free and most of all He gave us love
No love in all the world can compare
Not an artist on Earth could paint a picture like He
The trees in the autumn and flowers in spring
How lovely it is to hear the birds sing
If only the world was again at peace
The noise of gunfire and bombs would cease
It seems so wicked to kill and destroy
When He gave up His only boy
To save us all from evil and sin
One day we will wake from our dream
He will be there to welcome us in
His hands outstretched for us to hold
God's love for us is more precious than gold

D Gilson

THROUGH THE EYES OF A CHILD

The day is all new,
as the sun comes shining through.
There are so many things to do,
so many sights to view.

The green grass tickles the toes,
the fragrance of flowers delight the nose.
To catch a butterfly as it hovers over a rose,
such pleasure a child knows.

Raindrops to feel cool against the skin,
watermelon juice as it trickles down the chin.
Racing with your best friend or near kin,
trying your best to win.

Games to play,
throughout the day.
Others to become along the way,
oh, what delight! might I say.

Childhood days are too few,
when our life we view.
If only we could renew,
that wonderment before our life is through.

Linda Constantatos

SKEGNESS

I had to attend to some business in Scunthorpe one day last week,
So I drove down the coast to Skegness to take a little peek
At the resort I remembered from my childhood days,
With its Pleasure Beach and little winding waterways,
Bracing sea air and majestic clock tower,
The Fairy Dell that was my favourite bower.
As a kid I stood under the fountain and splashed in the bright blue pool
Wearing of a knitted swimsuit made of yellow wool.
It sounds bizarre but it was the latest trend,
My gran knitted it from a pattern she found in 'People's Friend'.
Pleasure Beach thrills were gained from the Haunted House,
Or for the very brave, a ride on the rickety Wild Mouse.
We had fish and chips in Sammy Seal's restaurant of glass,
All washed down with a tin of Shandy Bass.
Long gone are the places where I used to play,
The bits I remember have faded away.
Skegness of today is no longer quaint,
It's all steel and concrete, flashing lights and bright paint.
Even the clock tower seems pathetic and small,
Another seaside town that has lost its soul.

Megan Ward

I Remember

I remember my school days and the teacher I had,
Well, my teacher in classroom was not really bad.
It was my head teacher, she loved singing best,
Each week in the hall she would sing with a zest.

Now it so happens that 'God' didn't give me a choice,
When He made me a person, He gave me no voice.
I could talk, I could prattle, yet not sing a note,
Head teacher, Miss Byres, thought this a big joke.

On three days a week she would sing with my class,
Yes, those were the days I would get a good thrash.
It was, 'Out of this classroom, you little pest',
She thought I would contaminate all of the rest!

This made me sad for I had broken no rule,
And when the day came for me to leave school,
She told me quite plainly I had not a chance,
To survive in this world, I could not advance.

Despite all her warnings on things I would rue,
I remembered this dragon as the days slowly flew.
I came out victorious without singing a note,
No Prima Donna! But verse I have wrote.

Joan Prentice

THE OLD IFORD BRIDGE

The old stone bridge is incessant
With reflections remarkable, pleasant.
Thrill of winning a prize at the fair,
Caused merry laughter, filling the air.

The children eating their sweet, juicy toffee apples,
Were always a joy to see.
We went on a bus,
And went on a riverboat without any fuss!

In those days our accents were Hampshire born,
Now we all have a name proudly worn!
Transposed to Dorset where we now cling -
The old bridge still stands whate'er weathers bring!

Sammy Michael Davis

COUNTRY SCHOOLBOY
(Ireland 1940)

Down tree-lined lane I skip my way,
Delighting in a bright new day.
Skylark warbles in lofty blue,
Honeysuckle still wet with dew.
Hedgerow hums with bumblebee,
Cuckoo calls from far-off tree.
Dog rose pink with sunny smile,
Watch lizard basking for a while.
Pause again at roadside spring,
Play fingers in its crystal stream.
In the wood the blackbird sings,
At crossroads forge the anvil rings.
From a field the cattle stare,
Rural odours now in the air.
Passing by the farmyard gate,
Bruce, the dog, comes out to greet.
The big Shire horse nods his hello,
Pat his nose, then on I go.
Farm machine some fields away,
Horse-drawn reaper cutting hay.
Place wild flowers by holy well,
Linger by the old ruined mill.
Lean over bridge, see minnow play,
And wish there was no school today.
But alas, go through youth's prison gate,
And punishment for being late.

Terry O'Reilly

HAYMAKING

The early summer sun shone strong
the air resounded with the feathered warbler's song
I stand alone on a mound
near the earthen ring fort and gaze around
the grassy mantles and limestone plains
splendid in the absence of recent rains
the man in his shirt sleeves
wielded the scythe
doirníns gripped absorbed
skilfully mowing the grasses that waved in the breeze
swath after swath it lay inert on the ground
stopping now and then
sharpening stone in callused hand
the steel of the blade reflecting the sweat accrued
on his brow
the fragrance of new-mown hay
abiding in the caverns of my mind.

Bernadette McQuaid-Murphy

FANTASIES DON'T BREED MEMORIES

You've got to admit it, you've no chance,
With the best looking lass in the school,
Go on, be a fool, ask her to dance,
A refusal, a broken dream so cruel.

So why is it you have no memories
Of summer days and gorgeous lasses?
Because you got yourself stuck in your fantasies,
You've got to remove your rose-tinted glasses.

Fantasies don't breed memories,
You've got to lower your standards, somewhat!
Reality is what you have got to see,
Plenty of fish in sea in case you've forgot!

So she has great hair and oh so slim,
And she has a complexion so divine,
Putting it bluntly, you'll never get in,
Not within your lifetime or mine!

They are beautiful and they know it,
A hideous character beneath silky skin,
They want to be treat like royalty, don't I know it!
Punks like us would never ever fit in!

Fantasies don't ever breed memories,
You've got to change some of the scenery,
Add some durability for what you cannot see,
Bite your lip, get on with it, just like me!

Get it in your head, beauty is only skin deep,
The beauties on TV are not real!
If she hides the fat and the whiskers,
And what you don't know and what you don't feel,
Pretend she is 10 pounds lighter and cellulite free,
And those memories would grow continuously!

Darren Hobson

FRIENDS DEPARTED

Just to be near you,
  To see you and hear you,
    The sound of your round, clear voice.
      The gems so rare
        In your sparkling eyes,
          The sunbeams you stole for your hair.

For such as these we do grieve,
  When dear friends leave.
    We cherish the day you came.
      Our candle of mem'ries of you, will burn,
        With a gold immortal flame.

Dorothy Mary Allchin

GERALDINE'S MEMORIES

Happiness and playful days are memories I recall,
Punch and Judy, Crackerjack and nursing my favourite doll.
One hundred lines for doing wrong and a knuckle on my head,
Nibbed pens, inkwells, look at the books I must have read!
Swinging on the lamp post, skipping to a song,
Playing house, all dressed up, my friends would play along.

Mud pies and catching worms, rap the doors and run,
Cowboys and Indians, my brother had the gun.
Blind man's buff, pillow fights, pea shooters made me cry,
Jumping off the old shed roof, thinking that I could fly.

Andy Pandy, The Flowerpot Men, Willim the silly cat,
Skates and scooters, a ball, not forgetting the cricket bat.
Hallowe'en and Christmas time were my favourite times of year,
Going to church at Easter with all my finest gear.

Frilly dresses, straw hats, shoes with open toes,
Ribbons of different colours made into fancy bows.
Teddy bears and pussy cats, dolls and golliwogs,
Wellie boots in water, trying to catch the slimy frogs.

Painted faces with lipstick, eye shadow and Mum's powder,
Shouting with my brother to see if I could shout louder.
Walking walls, handstands, tumbling myself right round,
Making my first communion where I received my first pound.

Plastic shoes and bobby socks held up with an elastic band,
Seashores, seaweed, shells and lovely sand.
Mary Quant, Chubby Checker, not forgetting Peter Noone,
Dusty Springfield, Petula Clarke
And the first men on the moon.

These are my memories of days gone by
That no one can take away,
I'll tell them to my children's children
And pass them down the way.

Geraldine McMullan Doherty

THE BALLAD OF WALHAM GREEN
(With acknowledgements to James Elroy Flecker)

We used, as children, long ago,
The streets of Walham Green,
To play beneath the street lamp's glow,
Or in the summer sheen.

Ours was a happy childhood, free
From adult thoughts and ways,
We heedless played with childish glee
In pre and wartime days.

A whip and top, and hopscotch set
Upon the pavement grey,
Were 'mongst the games we'll not forget,
But think of still today.

And we could walk to Common Brook,
The roundabouts to ride,
To swap and read a comic book
Or brave the daring slide.

Our childhood's gone, but memories stay;
Through rosy glasses seen,
The games, the gangs, the ghosts who stray
The streets of Walham Green.

Jo Brookes

MEMORIES

We no longer see the reaper
Bronzed, muscular and lithe
Opening out the cornfields
With his great long bladed scythe.

To make way for the binder
By three great horses drawn
As it trundled along, it felled and sheaved
The long strawed golden corn.

About 5pm the farmer's wife
In the harvest field would appear
Bearing a huge butter basket of food
Tea urn, and home-brewed beer.

Oh well I remember those sandwiches
Of thick cut home-fed ham
And those golden pastried raspberry pies
And tarts crammed with home-made jam.

We no longer see stooks ripening
Or have harvest teas in the August sun
Or see men, and horses coming home from the fields
Tired, content, day's work well done.

E D Bowen

Margate - 1946

After the war to the seaside and barbed wire still on the beach,
An icy sea on the shingle . . . where a dark mine squats like a leach.

The merry clown brings the ices and dances in the rain,
His feet are quick and nimble and the dreams are real again.

After the war to the seaside! 'A proper one this year'
And a grey channel rain is sleeting and the arcade is shut on the pier.

But the merry clown goes laughing and leaps the rail with ease
And somersaults back for laughter - anything just to please.

Our landlady sports a black eye, yet old and prim as can be
Sits us in her cold parlour with cold toast and chaffy tea.

And my clown puts on a moustache, a shred of fringe from the chair,
And the child is bent with laughter and the dreams stay richly there.

With cold toast in the pocket to feed the shrilling gull,
A year's savings in the thin wallet, just waiting for rains to lull.

And we sit there in the shelter, wrapped up against the wind,
The child wedged in the middle and the drops on the roof are dinned.

Some dog has left a heap there and we watch a while and laugh
As wet people jump or scatter or shriek and make a splatter.

And the clown paints our holiday in rare and lovely hues
Margate after the war time - dream's sunshine held no blues.

Marian F Delfgou

AT PLAY IN YESTERDAY

Zulus in pampas grass plumes
That give away their position
To small boys in school caps
On their African expedition

Creeping through the tall grass
Catties drawn and loaded
A whispered one, two, three
Zulu head-dresses exploded

Tabby cat lying in the sun
Becoming tiger on the prowl
Another shot on target
Tiger lets out a howl

With the African sun blazing down
On grass-stained knees in shorts
The boys take a powwow
To gather in their thoughts

From a well-used Corona bottle
Each boy takes his slug of pop
Warm lemonade crystals
Bought from the corner shop

Passing train becomes charging elephant
Brave lads don't run away
Although it could become a dragon
When pretending another day

Now armed with sapling assegai
They trek off homeward bound
Animal magic on telly tonight
Mr Whippy van coming around

I R Finch

CHILDHOOD MEMORIES

I remember the days of my childhood, with a mixture of sadness
                                                                       and glee
And I remember the things we got up to, my friends and especially me.
Sometimes we'd play at the top of the pit
If Mother had known, she'd have thrown a blue fit.
We'd slide down the coal tips until we were black,
Then fall in the river on our way back.
We'd stay catching fish for a couple of hours,
Then think of poor Mam and pick her some flowers.
Go into Sam's orchard if he wasn't about,
If he came back and caught us, he'd give us a clout.
Saturday night, in would come the tin tub,
In front of the fire, we'd all get a scrub.
Then Mam sang us songs about really sad things,
Like little girls dying and angels with wings.
Sunday on the radio, was 'Journey Into Space',
And if you dared to make a sound, brother flicked you in the face.
Monday night, we all went to the pictures, it was nine pence
                                                           to get a hard seat,
I'd wriggle around to get comfy and land up with cramp in my feet.
The rest of the week, similar things went on,
It's sad now to think that these days are all gone.
But it will remain in my memory, how things used to be,
For my childhood friends, and especially me.

Alison Czajkowski

COCO SCHOOL

Let's go back to the days at school
Did you ever disobey the rule?
The Coco school, the first for me
No nursery in them days you see
Went on the back of my mother's bike
The other side of town was some hike
The bike with high handlebars and big wheels
With big straight frame of shiny steel
A message carrier on the back
With a tied cushion going slack
Then I had to sit very still
Especially turning at the wood mill
I remember the day of the summer show
Twenty-six small tots ready to go
Eight arrived in coloured paper dresses
With eight mothers in various stresses
Some because the colour's not right
One for the dress is far too tight
A minuet it was said to be
The parasol the best for me
Turned the wrong way to the right
Tripped the one with the dress too tight
Caused a bit of a stir I fear
When she ended up in tears
Her liberty bodice could be seen
While from her mother's ear came steam
Lucky next term I was off to school
Soon to play it by the rule.

Muriel Mackay

MEMORIES PAST AND PRESENT

Thinking back to my younger family days,
As a family, growing up together,
Happy, sad, whatever the weather,
At home or school, playing happy days,
Mam, Dad, two brothers, two sisters and me,
We had many a good time as a family,
Mam and Dad are now together above,
They showed us all how to love,
A few years later, we carried on doing our best,
Looking to future days, have been bless'd,
Learning to know right from wrong,
Hearing your children sing a song,
As a Christian, trying to help many others,
We are all like sisters and brothers,
The present age has changed, I can say,
Look to 'Jesus', the life, the truth, the way,
As I walk, talk to people, do a good deed,
Remember, be thankful, sow good seed.

Many happy memories, past and present.

Leslie Trotter

CHILDHOOD

My childhood days were 'Once upon a time',
With fairy tale beings and nursery rhymes,
The tooth fairy came and Santa Claus too,
I believed in their magic, but now, Harry who?
Potter I'm told is the lad's second name,
How quickly his character jumped into fame.
In my day the villain was some bogeyman,
Scary enough, with Desperate Dan,
The hero in comics, the Beano and such,
Somewhat exciting, but never too much.
Most reading matter the young pick up now,
Tends towards violence, frightening and how.
Never the bravest, afraid of the dark,
A brother who traded on this for a lark,
I remember now when they put out the light,
Hid under the bed clothes and shut my eyes tight.
Looking back now, recalling those fears,
Which seemed so enormous and drove me to tears,
And think, nowadays, with the power of TV,
How scared the more timid of youngsters must be.
Little doubt that this is a fact,
And any bravado is just a big act.
Do *not* steal their childhood, age comes soon enough,
The world they inherit is more than just tough.

Ellen Thompson

MY BROTHER TOM

I remember in 1930 when I was only four
My brother, Tom, without his cap when out the door
Off to school he went that hot summer's day
It was to be the last time he walked that way

Because of his illness, Tom was confined to his chair
And to go to bed he had to be carried up the stairs
His school inspector came to see why he was at home
But he found Tom was unable to walk across the room

In his wheelchair, Mother took him up the green lane one day
We came across a nest of partridges on our way
Mother picked one up for Tom to hold to his delight
We left the partridges, the smile on Tom's face was a worthy sight

Then came that fateful Monday morning, early in the day
Mother went upstairs, she cried out, oh Tom, he had just passed away
Sister Ellen went on the back of Martin's motorbike to tell Father
He hurried home on his push bike some time later

Tom was in the spare bedroom and in a coffin placed
I would go to see him when Mother asked me just to see his face
I had to say goodbye as off to church they went
My parents not wanting me to see Tom buried was their intent

Flowers on the grave, small garden at the side
Father kept everything neat and tidy, his grief he could not hide
Tom died from sunstroke, he was only seven
May we meet again dear brother, if I ever get to Heaven

Harry Skinn

SISTERS

Can you remember, Carole, when we were two little girls?
You with your pigtails and me with my curls.
We played together and fought together then we would call a truce.
Can you remember the pets we had and our dog called Bruce?
I was a little fattie but you were quite petite.
Can you remember all the years we lived on Prospect Street?
Can you remember the gas lamp that stood at the end of the street
And Durkin's shop on the corner where we bought our sweets?
Grandma and Grandad lived at number 4, Auntie Doris at number 8,
We lived at number 7, the one with the garden gate.
Can you remember the holidays we took with Mum and Dad
And the year we went to Jersey on the roughest crossing
They'd ever had?
Holidays in Cornwall and the Isle of Wight,
Uncle Tom's cabin in Blackpool and the illuminations, what a sight.
Can you remember going to Grandma's on a baking day,
Flat currant cakes and sweet loaves she baked upon a tray.
Taking turns to scrape the bowl, the palette knife and wooden spoon,
Those were good and happy times, no days were filled with gloom.
Can you remember the day you rode your first two-wheeler bike?
When you got tangled in the barbed wire fence, my you were a sight.
You and Mum in the kitchen when you tried on your first bra,
I spied on you through a peep-hole and you really got uptight.
Kiss-catch, tig, and hide and seek were a few games that we played,
We were so young and happy then, they were such happy days.
Can you remember the air raid shelters where we
Used to play and hide?
They were so damp and dirty and really dark inside.
Remember all the Easter eggs Gran sent us every year
And the lovely Christmas puddings filled with
Sixpences and Courvoisuer?
All these things I will treasure forever and I hope that you will too,
When the day God gave out sisters I am so glad He gave me you.

Valerie Walton

CHILDHOOD SUMMERS

Mum and Dad working hard in the café,
Isi and I packed off to Cornwall,
Grandparents eagerly waiting our coming,
Them and we would have a ball!

Par was the closest beach to their house,
(Our home in Bognor Regis was very far!)
We'd walk there and catch a bus back,
Gran and Grandad didn't have a car.

Carrying a tin full of home-made pasties,
A drink of lemonade and saffron cake,
Home-grown vegetables later on for tea,
And gorgeous butter and cream Gran would make.

Par was the beach we'd practice swimming,
Having been taught by Granny's friend,
Lying on top of a piano stool,
He'd show us how arms and legs to bend.

Cousins, down from Plymouth for the day,
Would meet us on Par sand,
Cricket was such fun to see,
Aunts and uncles lending a hand.

How we loved our trips to Fowey,
On the boat trip to river and sea,
And to Mevagissey, pretty place,
To go and catch mackerel for our tea.

Picking blackberries was another treat,
Purple stained hands and poorly belly!
Gran would then cook them up,
In pies, crumbles, jam and jelly.

On Fridays it was into St Austell,
The library, market, fish and chip lunch,
Oh what a time we had each summer,
We loved the whole time oh so much!

Jane Otieno

CHILDHOOD HOLIDAYS

A funny thing just happened to me
Whilst I was away on holiday
It involved a scene and me and my memory

Sitting on a bus going to the hotel
Parents fought with their children who were enduring hell
They complained and moaned, fidgeted, and never ceased to yell

Passengers annoyed, including me, were sighing
Ungrateful, selfish, spoilt brats, always crying
If I said I did not despise their whining I would be lying

Those poor parents probably worked and slaved for fifty weeks a year
To give good times and bonding by bringing all their family here
For childhood's end is always near and parents must accept
                                                    the loss they fear

My dislike for those ungrateful kids did grow
They think such times are forever and it goes by so slow
But looking back, this is untrue - that's one of the few things
                                                    that I know

Then a moment granted me an insight
For my parents also made such effort and sacrifices in their plight
When planning our holidays they were preparing to see
                                                their children's delight

Yes, the sight was a scene in my memory
For the children I scolded were, many years ago, me
I thought of my folks and I cried and felt guilty

Now I long to return and relive each childhood holiday
I would not grumble at petty things but enjoy, live and fulfil each day
For they soon pass by and are mourned the further they go away

Childhood holidays are things against which no other can measure
So enjoy them, give yourself and loved ones the pleasure
As childhood holidays when enjoyed can become memories
you'll treasure

Colin Jones

TOWN HALL PARK

All the kids in our neighbourhood,
Came to the park and it was good,
Challenging each other to do many things,
Stand on the roundabout, jump off the swings,
This is the place where our childhood went,
Where all of our spare time was spent.

Standing balanced on rocking horse seat,
Trying to stay there, past records to beat,
Climbing the wrong way up the slide,
Turn at the top and back down glide,
Until the town hall clock struck eight,
Then run home quick and don't be late.

Lots of land giving plenty of space,
To kick balls hard and run and race.
Shoving me up into horse chestnut tree,
Once I'd got the ball they'd forget me.
Playing football, boys and girls together,
All quite oblivious to the weather.

Playing cowboys and Indians, covered in mud,
Exercising our imaginations, lucky we could.
Very early courting up a tree,
If you want to get down, then kiss me.
Where do they spend their time today?
Where are the parks for the children to play?

Government offices took some ground,
Now only a toddlers' play area is found,
Doctors' surgery and a courthouse took the rest,
As children, I believe, we had the best,
Nowadays when I look around me,
'Ball games prohibited' is what I see.

P S D MacArthur

BETTER THAN

Two little boys were playing
Out in the street one day,
As I stood there watching,
I heard the little on say,

'Well, my dad's bigger than your dad,
And he's much stronger than yours.'
'Well, my dog's better than your dog,
And he's got bigger paws.'

As they stood there arguing,
I reflected back in time,
When my friend once said to me,
That his mum was better than mine.

So I gave a little giggle,
To think they fight the same old way.
At least that hasn't changed since I grew up,
Not like other things in life today.

Lynn Mottram

CHILDHOOD MEMORIES

Didn't have much in a material sense,
What we had cost only a few pence.
Made our own games of hide and seek,
Walked many miles, tired, hungry and weak.
Walking on tins made from old rope,
Scrumping in orchards, oh what a dope.
A few pence bought us some fags to share,
Smoking behind haystacks, we didn't have a care.
Our families worked hard to give us some treats,
We earned our pocket money to buy our sweets.
Many things to do from morning till night,
The farm work was busy, had to keep things right.
Only a young girl ploughing the fields,
Hoping a good crop is what it yields.
It was a better world then than we live in today,
The violence, the drugs, unheard of I'd say.

Audrey Davies

THE SATURDAY PENNY

What a wonderful coin was the Saturday penny,
It could buy you some sweet treats, the shop had so many.
Mr Reid, the shopkeeper, would greet us and say,
'Now what would you like with your penny today?
I've liquorice in pipes and in rolls with a sweet,
Jelly Babies, or rosebuds or toffee's a treat.
Dear lips and choc nuts or some pear drops to try,
I'm sure there is something that you'll want to buy.'
We would 'um' and then 'ah', there were always so many
Enticing bright sweets you could buy for a penny.
We would choose and then leave with two bags, quite content,
That our Saturday penny was very well spent.

Margaret B Baguley

THE ARCHES

The arches of Ravenscourt Park
Of my early life played a big part
Sand pit and sun
We were there to have fun
Although inside the arches were dark

The noise of the children echoed inside
On swing, roundabout, and on slide
We were protected from rain
While playing our game
They were brilliant places to hide

The trains rumbled on overhead
So you could never hear what was said
It was our special place
With plenty of space
But a place where a few tears were shed

The arches of Ravenscourt Park
Have definitely left their mark
I can remember the joys
But I can't hear the noise
Of us in Ravenscourt Park.

The arches of Ravenscourt Park
Where reality was never a part
Where we hatched our schemes
Our world was just dreams
Under the arches of Ravenscourt Park.

B Page

WHERE HAVE ALL THE DAYS GONE?

Where have all the days gone
The days when I had fun
Where have all the days gone
The days when I was young

Where have all the trees gone
The trees I used to climb
Where have all the trees gone
The trees I thought were fine

Where have all the birds gone
The birds that flew so high
Where have all the birds gone
The birds that ruled the sky

Where have all my dreams gone
The dreams that were so bright
Where have all my dreams gone
The dreams that bought me light

Where has all the love gone
The love that makes you glow
Where has all the love gone
I wish we all could show

I wish we all could show
The love that makes you glow
The love that makes you glow
I wish we all could show.

Where have all the days gone
The days when I had fun
Where have all the days gone
The days when I was young

Kerri Morehu-Baker

SAUSAGES

As kids, my brother Phil and I
Were sent into the town to buy
Some sausages from Mr Wood,
Whose sausages were always good.
Instead of going straight back home,
As children will, we chose to roam,
And looking for my brother's pal,
We found ourselves by the canal.

My brother, as we watched a boat,
Stuffed the bangers up his coat,
And for a joke, said with a grin,
'The sausages have fallen in!'
As he said this, he slipped and fell,
The sausages slipped out as well,
And to our very great dismay,
We watched and saw them float away.

What tragedy! What could we do?
But Phil with inspiration flew
Straight to the boat hire man close by,
A call for help his plaintive cry.
The kind man launched a sleek canoe
Retrieved the pack without ado,
Re-wrapped the sausages with care,
He was the answer to our prayer.

We ran straight home, said not a word
Although our sense of guilt was stirred.
The sausages were duly cooked,
Our crime, we thought, was overlooked.
The meal was eaten, no one died,
What luck! With what relief we sighed.
Then our neighbour called, she'd heard,
And told our Mum what had occurred.

Jax Burgess

THE STREET WHERE I WAS BORN

In the street here I was born
Looked like a picture in a book
Horse and cart on cobbled road
So many people where you look

So many shops down both sides
Each one was full of light
It's like going to a movie show
If you walked down in the night

Ladies' skirts down to the ground
Walking sticks and tall top hats
Lots of dogs all running free
Just chasing alley cats

The street's now gone so long ago
Just a memory of the time
That's in the street where I was born
Such good memories, they are mine.

A F Mace

THOUGHTS FROM CHILDHOOD

We walked to school through country lanes,
If misbehaved we had the cane;
We learnt our tables off by heart,
When school did play we all took part.

To Sunday School each week we went,
In Cubs and Scouts, to camp in tent;
We cleaned our shoes and made our bed,
We stayed at home till we were wed.

We did some work upon the farm,
We cut the thistles, kept from harm;
We walked to shop to post the letters,
We stayed at home till we were better.

We loved our cat, our dog and hens,
We dug the earth inside the pens;
Dear Reynard prowled for food for cubs,
Dear Brock scratched garden and upset tubs.

To village hall we went for whist,
We loved a walk in real thick mist;
When calf was due we went with Dad,
To pull and help to make all glad.

Some flowers and nuts each year we got,
Dear Mum soon put them in a pot;
The village policeman walked his beat,
If we worked hard we had our treats.

No foreign travel came our way,
To local seaside, each year, one day;
We loved the country, quiet and still,
We loved our parents, dear Florrie and Bill.

John Paulley

THE GOOD OLD BAD DAYS

My father was a miner,
At the pit all day.
Working hard to feed us,
With very little pay.

I was a very happy child,
With my four sisters and a brother.
No books, no shoes, no toys,
Just our love for one another.

Slept top to toe the four of us,
Having very little space.
Didn't seem to get much sleep
With a foot stuck in my face.

Newspaper spread across the table,
We would sit and eat our broth.
We all enjoyed our meals,
While we read the tablecloth.

We all seemed to laugh a lot,
And having lots of fun.
Never seemed to rain much,
Only playing in the sun.

Seventy years have passed,
Our lives have been quite good.
Would we have ever changed it?
You bet your life we would.

B Cotterill

SEEMS LIKE YESTERDAY . . .
(Dedicated to my big sister - 'friends and enemies')

It's funny just how sometimes
When I'm sitting all alone
The memories come flooding back
And I feel like running home

So young and free we were back then
We didn't have a care
Two girls, two friends, two enemies
We had a lifetime to share

You taught me how to finger-knit
To walk on wooden stilts
How to win at marleys
A friendship then was built

We spent hours playing with Pippa dolls
And balls shoved into tights
You let me share your bed, if I
Was ever scared at night

You called me names that hurt me
And still I came back for more
I was happy to walk in the shadow
Of the sister I adored

I'll never forget my fear
As you chased the school bully away
For blood is thicker than water, and
I knew you loved me that day

But overnight we grew up fast
And then we grew away
It's funny how you don't miss time
Until it's slipped away

It feels a million years have passed
As memories start to fade
Yet when I'm sitting all alone
It seems like yesterday . . .

Jo-Ann Waldron-Hall

CHRISTMAS EVE

Father Christmas was my hero
When I was a child,
I thrilled to think him riding
Through the winter night so wild.

My parents encouraged this belief
At four and five and six,
'Tho secretly they'd be glad to be rid
Of Santa and his tricks.

They must have felt quite weary
When I still believed at seven,
Getting up at crack of dawn
Was not their idea of Heaven.

When I was eight I did begin
To have some horrid doubts,
There were whispers in the playground
Beneath the children's shouts.

I broached it with my parents
And they exchanged a glance,
To have a peaceful Christmas eve -
This could be their chance.

'Is there a Father Christmas?'
I really did persist,
My mother breathed a deep sigh,
'Yes dear, he does exist.'

'There is no Father Christmas,'
At nine I told my mother.
'Yes, you are quite right, dear,
Just don't tell your little brother.'

Gaye Gatehouse

BIG HEAD

Way back in the fifties, when I was a little lad
I came home from school one day, very, very sad
Mum just rubbed my hair and said, 'What's the matter boy?
Tell me what's upset my little bundle full of joy.'
'The kids all call me big head and take the micky out of me.'
Mum said, 'Just ignore them, and they'll stop it, wait and see.
Now be a good boy and run up to the shops,
I need ten pounds of spuds and half a dozen chops.'
'Okay Mum,' I said, 'have you got a bag to carry that?'
'Oh no, I haven't son, just shove 'em in your hat.'

Esmond Hannon

THIS GAME

I remember at the age of three or four
the excitement began as we came through the door,
we'd begin to look around
as we hung up our coats,
from the rug to the lampshade
and the picture of boats.

Our eyes were alert as Mum put on tea
eager to be first, my brothers, sister and me.
We'd seek the upside down picture,
the lids swapped on the jars,
or spot different coloured bonnets
on the boys' tin cars.

You see Mum was our rock,
our teacher and guide,
who made our lives fun by
keeping our eyes open wide.

She'd spend just ten minutes
moving something around.
Making it simple so we knew
when it was found.

We'd squeal with delight
when we spotted the change,
and laugh when we thought
that it looked strange.

And the name of this game
we all loved to play?
'Twas simply,
Is there anything to notice today?

Rebecca Johnson

NIGHTMARES OF CHILDHOOD

They entered my world of somnolence
As the hands of the clock turned twelve
Taking my soul and my fragile mind
Into a world where ghosts do delve
I had hidden 'neath a sanctuary of blankets
Hoping sleep would escort my dread away
But the presence of my fear kept lingering
Forcing the whole of my consciousness to stay

The silence of the room was deafening
Darkness hung like a suffocating cloud
The night seemed to stop and smile at me
Being imprisoned in its nocturnal shroud
Creaking floorboards announced their presence
Shadows rode on the essence of my doom
The wind whistled against the cowardly windows
As the whispers poured into the room

Figures rose from their habitual sarcophagus
Creeping into the corners of my eyes
I saw the faces of night's godless sentinels
Who stare back from reality's demise
The spirits of the dead tormented me
Touching the soul of my sleepless dream
Thus I retreated 'neath the soft warm blankets
And from my sanctuary came a mortified scream

After the dramatic nightmares of childhood
That are replaced by adulthood jest
The visitations of one's primal imagination
Are childhood memories we never forget

David Bridgewater

SWEET SHOP DOWN THE LANE

The sweet shop down the lane
Was the memory I can recall
My Saturday morning treat
When I was very small.

Clutching 'ten pennies' in my hand
I raced eagerly down the hill
Entering the shop at a terrific pace
Skidding to a halt by the till.

A smile from behind the counter
From the 'sweetie lady' as she was known
Surrounded by a sickly aroma of fudge
I was lost in a world of my own.

Gazing at endless rows of sweets
I never knew which ones to buy
The 'sweetie lady' always sensing this
Handed me sugared delights to try.

She knew my favourite were 'flying saucers'
A bitter sherbet wafer thing
Followed by the 'sherbet fountain'
With sticky liquorice string.

Tempting chocolates, lemon sherbets
Coconut pyramids, pineapple cubes
Aniseed twists, penny chews
Candy necklace and 'Smarties' in tubes.

From the silver scales into candy-striped bags
I watched as my sweets she did pour
Thirty years on and I still have this dream
To visit that sweet shop once more!

Louise Mawbey

Covert Boyhood

At nine years old, a double life I led
With secret knowledge locked inside my head.
For weeks on end I worried what I said;
My information made me status red.

At school I daily would avoid the boys
In case they saw through my defensive poise.
Instinctively I sensed their raucous noise
Might badger out my secret with their ploys.

In isolation I would roam the field,
Spend hours alone to harbour, never yield
My precious secret in my head concealed:
Disaster would ensue if I revealed.

Expansive grasslands were my haunt compressed
As furtively, a little boy obsessed,
Beneath big skies I lay quite prepossessed
And unseen, savoured what I then possessed.

Throughout that spring it was my constant quest
To play my cards close to my little chest.
If I told one, he'd just tell all the rest
That deep in the grass I'd found a skylark's nest!

Patrick Brady

TINS, TAMBOURINES AND A BIG BASS DRUM

As I gazed at an old photo of my mam and dad,
It nudged a heap of memories, some happy, some sad.
They are standing so proudly in their uniforms,
Memories of distant summers, when every day was warm.

Childhood memories of harsh and rigid discipline,
Wondering, what did it all mean?
Men, women and children in their own Citadel,
Fighting their Christian war against the infidel.

Children dressed up in their Sunday best,
Singing and praying along with the rest.
As you get older your perspective changes,
Suddenly you find your time rearranged.

Sunday mornings, tins shaking, band playing, a cacophony of sound,
You could hear them coming for streets all around.
Dad passionately wanted to play the big bass drum,
That was quite impossible, given the size of his tum.

The army was a large part of their lives,
A common bond that will always survive.
Sometimes we hold onto the strangest things,
Finding comfort in the solace that it brings.

David Muncaster

A CHILD'S WONDERLAND

On this, my magic carpet
I travel to wonderland
It's cool to be a child
Building castles in the sand

I imagine I've got wings
Above our planet fly
Skate down the rainbow
Painted in the sky

My face catches sunbeams
That sparkle, shimmer and shine
Jack Frost nips my toes
I catch snowflakes so fine

I pull a funny face
At the man in the moon
Hop from star to star
Dream of the land of Zoon

I blow the dandelion clock
And make a wish to be
To marry my prince charming
And sail across the sea

Like being on a sea-saw
My moods are up and down
You'll often find me laughing
Or maybe a cry or frown

At the bottom of my garden
I watch the fairies play
And hope these childhood memories
Are in my heart to stay

Patricia Carter

CHILDHOOD MEMORIES

How strange it is in our twilight years,
Memories flood back of joy and fears.
So distant, stretching far away,
Yet on recall seem like yesterday.

How we enjoyed our rides on the bus,
Sitting on top, never making a fuss.
If it rained, that was part of the fun,
An adventure it seemed had just begun.

Maybe we would go down to the sea,
To run and paddle and feel so free,
Or crowd round with others, to watch naughty Punch
Whacking poor Judy, and then go to lunch.

Sometimes off to the country we'd go,
Excited and feeling all aglow.
Collecting blackberries in a bright red tin,
Munching cucumber sandwiches, deliciously thin.

From an early age we always knew
That money was short, so 'I want' was taboo.
Somehow each Christmas was filled with good cheer,
We made paper chains off and on, through the year.

The front doorbell rings, I come back with a start,
My memories fade, and again I'm a part
Of the present, with everything moving apace,
No time for memories, just a frantic race
To where?

Kathleen Holmes

The Stream

Through the hills the stream meandered,
Cotswold water so pure and clean.
Down to the valley it wandered,
Flowing into lush, verdant green.

To a boy it meant adventure,
Attracted like a magnet.
Imagination without care,
Here fantasy and playtime met.

Swinging on tree vines like Tarzan,
Across croc-infested rivers.
Seek the source of the Amazon,
Like rugged famous explorers.

With rusty sieve panning for gold,
We're 'old timers' in the 'Wild West'!
Find fist-size nuggets to be sold,
'Lone Star' rifle is not for jest.

Like beavers we built large dams,
Then destroyed them with clay bombs!
Hot, lazy days with no aims,
We dangled feet with no qualms.

Oh to be a boy without a care,
With only 'bubblegum' to share.

Mike Curtis

70s Remembered

Crumpled woodbine packet
Black Harrington jacket
Levi stay press
Juvenile unruliness
White Fred Perry
White cider merry
Long heavy crombie
Rastafarian zombie
Dr Martin boots
White boiler suits
Clockwork Orange eyeliner
Blackened eye shiner
Yard long laces
Bright red braces
Scarves on wrists
Knuckle-duster fists
Girlfriend love bite
School club fight
Shiny new brogues
Inner city rogues

Martin Kerr

CHILDHOOD MEMORIES

I find myself hankering after the past,
When summers were warm and the sunshine would last.
Right up until supper we always had fun.
Living down on the farm there was work to be done.

We would work in the fields in the hours after school.
In the month of October 'twas always the rule
To have time off for harvest and help with the crops.
In the evenings we went to the socials and hops.

The music was good and the ballads as well.
These days we know it is so hard to tell
What these pop stars are saying, they all sound the same.
Their dress is outrageous and they're searching for fame.

We didn't have much in material wealth,
But we all seemed so happy, enjoying good health.
We walked everywhere, and we just didn't mind.
Then we progressed to cycling, come rain or come shine.

We went into church after Sunday School class.
By the time we returned, four hours had passed.
We never complained as it had to be done.
'Twas part of our lives in the midst of the fun.

It would seem now the world's in a terrible mess
Because God's laws are broken, no more and no less.
Nobody cares about how they behave.
We're paying the price - to sin we're enslaved.

Let's get back to the scriptures and heed what they say.
Get right with our Saviour - no further delay.
His patience wears thin, He will soon call the roll.
We must all make sure that it's well with our soul.

Maureen Anderson

SCHOOL BLUES

Sitting, thinking, writing an essay
Slowly falling asleep
Reading, thinking, answering questions
Quickly counting the sheep.

Reading, reading Shakespearean plays
Gradually feeling the pace
Staring, glancing at meaningless poems
Immediately losing the place.

Shouting, laughing, class reading books
Noisily keeps me awake
Slipping, drifting, sleep takes a grip
Quickly without mistake.

Sleeping, dreaming, visions of home
Gently come to my mind
Walking, talking, teacher approaches
Firmly kicks my behind.

I wake up . . .

Slowly rub my eyes
Quickly sit up straight
Gradually envisage
What will be my fate.

Immediately my answer
Noisily comes back
Quickly I look over
'The exercise for Black'.

Gently I receive it
Firmly tear it up
Must get back to sleep now
So everyone - shut up!

John Black

For My Nanny

My nanny died and we put her in the ground
It must be dark and lonely there, quiet without a sound
I watched my mammy silently, she cried and cried and cried
She said she was feeling sad because Nanny had died
A funny man said some words and then we all went back to
                                                        Nanny's house for tea
They all fussed around my mammy, they forgot all about me
I miss my nanny too and I want to know when she'll be coming back
I don't understand what's going on and what is a heart attack?
My mammy said that when people die they go to Heaven to
                                                        live with God
I tried to understand what she meant, smiled and gave my head a nod
My mammy smiled at me gently and kissed me on the head
But I'm going to ask God about my nanny when I say my
                                                        prayers in bed
I love you Nanny, but your being dead makes my mammy feel sad
Being dead can't be a good thing if it makes everyone else feel bad
I'm never going to die Nanny, because I don't want to make
                                                        my mammy cry
And I don't want to live in the ground, I thought Heaven was
                                                        up in the sky!

J Gatenby

THOSE HAPPY DAYS

Sink into your favourite chair
And think about the times that were
The happiest of your childhood days
And the joys you had in many ways.

The street you lived, a playground vast
Where games seemed to forever last,
And every day, or so it seemed
In clear blue skies the sunshine gleamed.

There came the times when rain clouds poured,
But never a moment to be bored,
With Snakes And Ladders and Ludo to play,
Or comics to read, just 'swapped' that day.

And when the heavy rain passed by,
What fun for every girl and boy,
While searching for sticks, one may utter,
'Let's race them down the 'flowing gutter'.

Street traders' handcarts held a prize
To attract your very eyes,
A goldfish or a lively chick
For a bundle of rags, you could take your pick.

Always eager, an errand to run,
A means to an end, to add to your fun,
It didn't take long for it to be learned,
By using the money that you had earned,

With your friends excitedly,
Hurriedly on your way you'd be,
To see your favourite hero soon
At the 'pictures' on Saturday afternoon.

The best times were the childhood days,
And rightly so, in many ways,
So when you look back, it's nice to declare
It wasn't a dream, you really were there.

Leslie Frank Checkley

THOSE BYGONE DAYS

Oh to go back to those bygone days
When summer's sunny, winter's snowy
Playing out all day in the fresh air,
Coming in, cheeks rosy and glowy,
Then sat around a big roaring fire
So to thaw out from the freezing cold,
With hot-aches in fingers and toes,
Eating hot chestnuts as stories told.
Next to the fire, a big black oven,
Oh the lovely smell as bread did bake,
Mum gave us dough to squeeze and roll
For shapes, tho' grubby to make.
There were no washing machines then,
Only dolly tubs, large, fat and round,
And brass posher with long handle
To posh and swing the clothes around,
And of course the scrubbing board,
Ribbed glass or metal with wood surround,
Later to be used in skiffle groups
Rubbed to make a most unusual sound.
Rationing over just after the war,
No sweets much to make our teeth bad
So dipped fingers in cocoa and sugar,
Or any concoction that was to be had.
We were very happy with make-believe,
No TV or modern toys,
Not many cars so could play 'tig'
In the street, a gang of girls and boys,
Whip and top was all the rage
To chalk lovely colours in bright swirls,
Then to whip the top like mad to see
The best pattern as it twirls.

No designer clothes then to wear,
Hand-me-downs were par for the course
Until ragged and torn to wait
For rag and bone man and his horse.
A gypsy came round to sharpen knives,
His foot up and down on the treadle,
Didn't like us getting too near,
Told to keep away and not to meddle.
Three times on Sunday to chapel went,
Shops closed, no games, quietly read,
After service, friends came for supper,
Had sing-song till time for bed.

Our parents kept from us
The hardship and strife,
Just gave us happy moments
For us to reminisce in later life.

Tess Walton

HUNSTANTON

Most of the year it was school and games.
I was happy; I loved to play.
Then would come a magical moment -
We're off to Hunstanton today!

I've packed my case, got my shrimping net.
Make sure you leave nothing behind.
It's 60 miles on a snorting train.
Chiddly chook, chiddly chook, says the line.

A whole two weeks to play on the beach,
To find starfish in the rock pools.
To swim in the sea (with a toe on the ground)
A deception which has nobody fooled.

To play French cricket and eat ice cream.
To go red and (hopefully) brown.
The blisters don't hurt much cos we're so brave.
We can cover up and go to town.

The day you go, a fortnight's forever.
This is life as it always should be.
Halfway through the next week it's different,
Somehow, home is calling to me.

I've loved my holiday, but I'm glad it's done
Though it isn't quite over yet.
I shan't be sorry to pack my case,
I'm missing my friends and my pet.

We travel home along with chiddly chook,
To pick up the reins of our being.
To live another 11½ months
Until Hunstanton again we'll be seeing!

Joyce M Jones

THE ROAD

Where does the road go to, Mummy?
I know I grew in your tummy.
Now, I am three
I can go and see
what is that hill
beyond the mill?

*All is so still
down by the mill.*
I run home to my mummy.
Oh, to be back in her tummy!

Kinsman Clive

LOST CHILDHOOD

Who walks into the garden green?
For many a day none has been seen
Except the gardener, old and grey,
Who burrows here from day to day
And plants sweet pinks and roses red
And candytuft in every bed,
But most he loves the soft stocks white
Which smell so sweetly in the night.

The mighty beech boughs lace the sky
And far below the long lawns lie.
Each gravel path is neatly made
But no one walks in the chestnut shade.
There works the gardener, old and grey
And grows more mole-like every day,
And there the crooked apple trees
Shed blossom gently in the breeze.

Diana Richardson

UNBORN

They never knew you, never touched you
but to me you were so real,
I spoke to you every day
every movement was a thrill.

You were my special love
a bond never to break
I looked after you so carefully
you were for no one else to take.

But the magic didn't last forever
it just wasn't meant to be
I did all I could to keep you
you should be here with me.

Don't worry, don't cry
there will always be another
but you're the one I wanted
I should have been your mother.

I never got to meet you
we never had the chance
but my baby you're in my dreams
we laugh and play and dance.

Still every day I remember you
and although we had to part
my child, I will love you forever
you are locked within my heart.

Sharon Simpson

THE BLUEBELL WOODS - MAY 1948

My sister woke me early, it seemed the break of day.
'Get up,' she said, 'you lazy bones, it's time we were away.'
I rubbed my fingers in my eyes, prepared to have a moan,
But then my memory was jogged by something in her tone.
Sleep now was quite forgot. I jumped out of my bed,
And with the most unseemly haste, dragged clothes on o'er my head.
My sister, laughing, buttoned me up and tied my belt behind,
Not crossly as on schooldays, but smiling, bright and kind.
She plaited my hair as tight as tight, I washed at the kitchen sink,
Then porridge oats for breakfast and hot sweet tea to drink.
The sun was shining brightly that morn in early May
As we slammed the door behind us and set out on our way.
Every gateway brought more friends, 'til we were quite a crowd.
Happy, smiling, carefree girls, we laughed and chattered loud.
Along the lane to town we went, across the market square,
Cheerfully greeting another group of girls who waited there.
Down the early morning streets the milkman watched us go;
His horse let out a friendly neigh as though he liked the show.
Mothers, scrubbing doorsteps, smiled to see us pass.
Curtains twitched at windows as some waved through the glass.
And so we reached the countryside with lovely sights to see,
The miles went by, we stopped to eat, jam pieces and cold tea.
Then the target of our trek, a rutted stony way
Which led us to the bluebell woods, the highlight of our day.
There, spread all around us in the dappled shade of spring,
A sight to lift our flagging steps and make our senses sing.
We happily ran among the trees, then resting on the ground
Feasted blissful eyes upon the sea of blue around.
Though we were many we showed restraint and picked the
                                            blooms with care,
For we knew they would flower another year if we only took a share.
The sun was now well past noon, time for home to head,
So thirsty, tired and dusty we our weary way did tread.
My sister held me by the hand, I walked as in a dream
Bluebells limp across my arm, heart and mind serene.

A drink of water at the farm, a toffee and a smile
Encouraged tired legs to stretch and walk another mile.
Throughout that day, no quarrels marred the happy sister band
And little girls who lagged behind soon found a helping hand.
The sun was near to setting when at last we reached the town
And with a 'tat-tah' and a 'see you soon', our numbers
                                                dwindled down.
I nodded at the table when we sat down to eat.
My father gently lifted me and set me on my feet.
He undressed me and washed me, tucked me up in bed;
And dreams of sun and bluebells drifted sweetly through my head.

Frances Marie Cecelia Harvey

REMEMBRANCE OF CHILDHOOD
(For Dave Austin: a dear friend and mentor)

Entrancing is the summer's breeze;
Its comforting embrace,
So gentle, warm and soft, as fays
That dance upon my face,
And dear, as 'tween the marching clouds,
Those fleeting boons of light;
Each momentary glimpse a hope
That promises as bright.

Enchanting is the babbling brook;
Its strange soliloquy,
That sends me to the fondest realms
Of sweet tranquillity:
Exciting! Like those hazy fields
Of buoyant early youth,
Where dewy-eyes, in fluffy skies,
Sought visionary truth.

O Blesséd! Blesséd are those days;
The sweet remembrance,
Of countless blissful whiling hours,
And childish innocence:
Of days when skies seemed twice their size,
And twofold bright the sun,
When one day seemed as twenty now,
And twenty times more fun.

Harry Crompton-Fils

AN INSIGNIFICANCE OF BEING

Sometimes a tear will fall when I reflect on a past
The years, how they did travel so fast

From childhood to adulthood I did embrace
Love, sorrow and death is a canvas we all face

A creation that was not to take a breath
Someone that was never understood even after death

Destruction and the survival of feuding nations
How long has man fought for a salvation?

What is the purpose for one to evolve
When the question of why we exist is never to be solved?

A picture of two cherubs appear
Reality of their fate everyone fears

This is a world we have made
Now there will always be a reason to be afraid

Anthony Ross-Fallon

CHILDHOOD HOLIDAYS

Sand and sea and glorious sun
Oh the pleasure and the fun!
To paddle in that turquoise sea
Then stroll down to the café for tea
Back to the beach to search for shells
Gaze into a pool where a creature dwells
Sitting on rocks to watch the waves
Then wander through those magic caves
While Mum and Dad doze in deck chair
And life goes on without a care
Oh those halcyon summer days
Of our childhood holidays!
Life was carefree and such fun
With days of never-ending sun
Back to the hotel to be bathed and fed
Then tucked up cosily in bed
Knowing that the following day
We once more will go out and play
On that glorious sandy shore
Oh to be that child once more!

Pat Rogers

THE SECRET

'No one will know that it's there.'
Though only seven, I was made to swear
That I never would reveal,
Not even to my friends, what I had to conceal
Beneath my clothes each day at school.
Times were hard, just after the war. There was no rule
To accompany children all of the time.
We did our best, committed no crime,
Pulled together, lived our lives as we must.
Youngsters matured fast with duty and trust:
Home first, I'd lay the fire and start the tea.
That's when I'd use my secret latchkey.

Valerie Catterall

I Don't Understand Why

Why does the moon in the sky float so high?
Why do the heavy clouds pass right on by?
Why don't the aeroplanes fall out of the sky?
Please - I don't understand why.

Why do the birds sing such different songs?
Why can't all people just 'get along'?
When things need to be right, why are they always wrong?
Please - I don't understand why.

If I don't understand; am I stupid as well?
Is my life on this Earth gonna be 'living hell'?
Should I end it right now, or be strong? - I can't tell
Please - I don't understand why.

Let me in, show me how, I just want a chance
I'm sure if you show me, I'd repeat that dance
I'd live for the moment if only to 'prance'
Please - I don't understand why.

I just want to help, to be part of the team
To see my potential and realise my dream
And if things aren't right and not what they seem
Please - I don't understand why.

I'll try very hard to play just by the rules
Just to be included and be nobody's fool
I'll keep my nose clean and act really 'cool'
Please - I don't understand why.

Let me be who I am, though I'm simple of wit
I'll not 'get in the way' just contribute a bit
Then I'll take a back seat and pretend I'm a hit!
Please - I don't understand why.

Sue Elle

ANCHOR BOOKS SUBMISSIONS INVITED
SOMETHING FOR EVERYONE

ANCHOR BOOKS GEN - Any subject, light-hearted clean fun, nothing unprintable please.

THE OPPOSITE SEX - Have your say on the opposite gender. Do they drive you mad or can we co-exist in harmony?

THE NATURAL WORLD - Are we destroying the world around us? What should we do to preserve the beauty and the future of our planet - you decide!

All poems no longer than 30 lines.
Always welcome! No fee!
Plus cash prizes to be won!

Mark your envelope (eg *The Natural World*)
And send to:
Anchor Books
Remus House, Coltsfoot Drive
Peterborough, PE2 9JX

OVER £10,000 IN POETRY PRIZES TO BE WON!

Send an SAE for details on our latest competition!